D1199298

Hello, America!

Alamo

by R.J. Bailey

Bullfrog
Books

Ideas for Parents and Teachers:

Bullfrog Books let children practice reading informational text at the earliest reading levels. Repetition, familiar words, and photo labels support early readers.

Before Reading
- Discuss the cover photo. What does it tell them?
- Look at the picture glossary together. Read and discuss the words.

Read the Book
- "Walk" through the book and look at the photos. Let the child ask questions. Point out the photo labels.
- Read the book to the child, or have him or her read independently.

After Reading
- Prompt the child to think more. Ask: Have you ever been to the Alamo? Did you take a tour? Did you see a battle reenactment?

Bullfrog Books are published by Jump!
5357 Penn Avenue South
Minneapolis, MN 55419
www.jumplibrary.com

Library of Congress Cataloging-in-Publication Data

Names: Bailey, R.J., author.
Title: Alamo / by R.J. Bailey.
Description: Minneapolis, Minnesota: Jump!, Inc. [2017] | Series: Hello, America! | Includes index.
Audience: Ages 5–8.
Identifiers: LCCN 2016008124 (print)
LCCN 2016008545 (ebook)
ISBN 9781620313473 (hardcover: alk. paper)
ISBN 9781624963940 (ebook)
Subjects: LCSH: Alamo (San Antonio, Tex.)—Siege, 1836—Juvenile literature.
Classification: LCC F390 .B35 2016 (print)
LCC F390 (ebook) | DDC 976.4/03—dc23
LC record available at http://lccn.loc.gov/2016008124

Editor: Kirsten Chang
Series Designer: Ellen Huber
Book Designer: Molly Ballanger
Photo Researcher: Molly Ballanger

Photo Credits: Alamy, cover, 18, 19, 22bl; Ben Grey/Flickr.com, 8; Corbis, 9, 20–21; Getty, 14–15; iStock, 3, 4, 10–11, 22br, 23bl; Jim Laux/Flickr.com, 6–7; Nagel Photography/Shutterstock.com, 23br; NeonLight/Shutterstock.com, 16–17; Shutterstock, 1, 5, 12–13, 22tl, 23tl, 23tr, 24; Thinkstock, 5, 23tr.

Printed in the United States of America at Corporate Graphics in North Mankato, Minnesota.

Table of Contents

Fight to Be Free

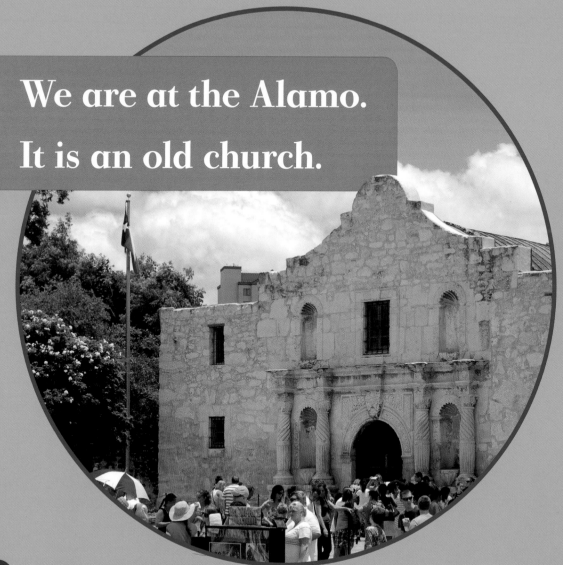

We are at the Alamo.

It is an old church.

It is in Texas.

We go inside.
It is quiet. Shh!

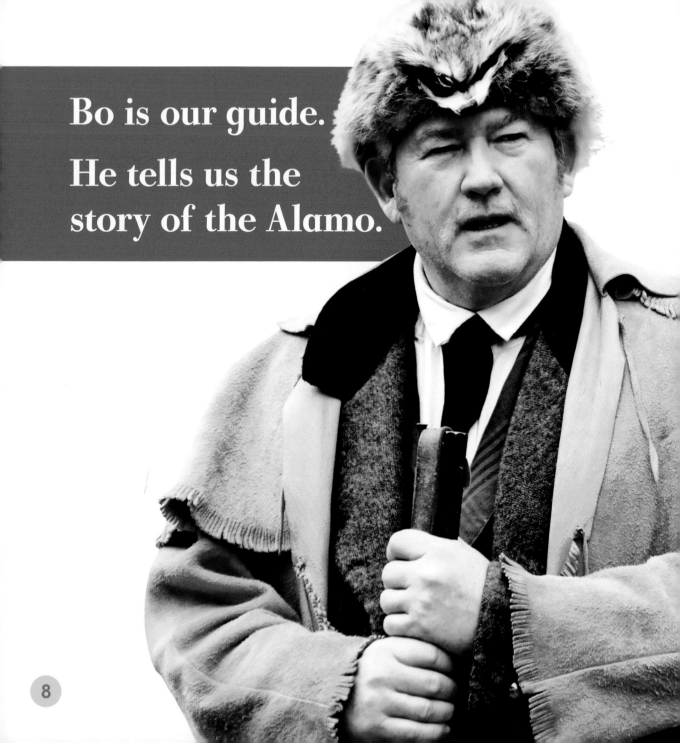

Bo is our guide.
He tells us the
story of the Alamo.

There was a fight here.
It was in 1836.

Texas was part
of Mexico.

But some Texans
wanted to be free.

TRAVIS

CROCKETT

11

12

They fought
Mexico's army.

It took 13 days.

The Texans lost.

But it was an important fight.

Soon Texas was free.

Today, men act
out a fight.

Boom!

It's OK.

It is not real.

It teaches us
about the past.

Nearby, we see a tomb. Who is buried there? Brave men.

They did not win.

But they gave others hope.

BOWIE

BONHAM

JOSEPH BAYLISS · JOHN BLAIR · SAMUEL C. BLAIR · WILLIAM BLAZEBY · JAMES BUTLER BONHAM · JAMES BOWIE · JESSE B. BOWMAN · DANIEL BOURNE · GEORGE BROWN ·
GEORGE WASHINGTON COTTLE · HENRY COURTMAN · LEMUEL CRAWFORD · DAVID CROCKETT · ROBERT CROSSMAN · DAVID P. CUMMINGS · ROBERT CUNNINGHAM ·
SHEROD J. DOVER · LEWIS DUEL · ANDREW DUVALT · CARLOS ESPALIER · GREGORIO ESPARZA · ROBERT EVANS · SAMUEL B. EVANS · JAMES L. EWING · WILLIAM FISHBAUGH ·
JOHN E. GASTON · JAMES GEORGE · JOHN CALVIN GOODRICH · ALFRED CALVIN GRIMES · JOSE MARIA GUERRERO · JAMES C. GWIN · JAMES HANNUM · JOHN HARRIS ·
WILLIAM D. HOWELL · WILLIAM D. JACKSON · THOMAS JACKSON · GREEN B. JAMESON · GORDON C. JENNINGS · LEWIS JOHNSON · JOHN JONES · JOHNNY KELLOGG · JAMES KENNEY ·

19

Remember the Alamo!

A Day at the Alamo

church

Texas flag

reenactment

monument

Picture Glossary

Mexico
A country that borders the state of Texas and other states.

Texas
One of 50 states in the United States; it became a state in 1845.

Texans
People who live in the state of Texas.

tomb
A place where people are buried.

Index

To Learn More

Learning more is as easy as 1, 2, 3.

1) Go to www.factsurfer.com

2) Enter "Alamo" into the search box.

3) Click the "Surf" button to see a list of websites.

With factsurfer.com, finding more information is just a click away.